The Cosmic Hello

C. Alexander

The Cosmic Hello ©2018 by C. Alexander.

All rights reserved. Printed in the United States of America.

First Edition. Edited by : Amy Youngmann and Julia Gordon-Bramer

Design by: jannatul138 on Fiverr

ISBN: **978-1987753448**

To friends, family, Michelle, and the twisted Muse assigned to me since birth

Research and Loss

Buying Psychic Abilities, Enlightenment, and Government Conspiracies

You came home spouting off about Aleister Crowley

and secret societies,

Lumerians and Atlantians and reptilian overlords.

"Those in power are already using this stuff;

we just need to know it too, to survive, to thrive."

And mostly I think you were just trying to impress the

dude you were fucking

behind my back. You used to cry when Mufasa died,

but now you feel nothing, nothing, nothing.

When did you become a false prophet?

genocidal attitudes towards closed minds,

but I think yours was too open,

some spilled out around your alien toes.

I don't know how to put it back in.

I think you ate my spirit. Devoured it and conquered it,

now I'm just shit,

growing mushroom clouds.

You wear your philosophy like a feathered boa.

You say things like, **"Oh I hope he notices my dharma"**
Please,

tell me more about the tapestry you bought.

Tell me more about the great golden Buddha statue

"It's made of real shiny rocks from under the ground!"

I see myself as a honey bee,

you're a vengeful hornet, stinging me for

walking too close to the sun-

flower beds (Most lilies are hardly lilies at all).

You're calling manatees (red headed) mermaids, and I'm a
drunk

sailor praying to a bottle, at least I can touch

my God.

Polly, like polyamorous

The porch swing was new. It was empty. The leather
strapped chairs were old. They were filled. With us and the
weight of who was not there. The cups held coffee. They
were not my cups. They were not your cups. You told me
you had been thinking about what it means to be honest and
if it mattered, and who it mattered to. You told me not to be
angry. You told me you were so sorry. You told me to stop
torturing myself with the details. I became aware of the keys
in my pocket. The ones that could easily get me away from
there. Then there was screaming. Then there was tossed
porch furniture. Then there was a long walk alone. Then
nothing.

Lemurians, Atlantians, Martians, and Why I Hate Anubis

Fox-like
or is it dog-like?
Soul stealing cameras create red-eyed
demons
or simply heterochromia.
Vlad the Impaler had white blood
cells and a reflection too.

Left-brained rightness cripples creativity.
Definitively defined dictionary terms on a blackboard
in a cave reflecting shadows
upon shadows upon shadows.
If I could just hold the smoke you blow in rings
in between
squarepegroundhole conversations and false kisses,
I might know something more about the fabric
of reality.

I might know more about the fabric
of dreaming,
as the fabric of my bedsheets rub against
unfamiliar legs,
and the fabric of my legs rub against
unfamiliar legs.

You say: **"we're all just clawing our way
towards enlightenment,
one lifetime at a time."**
And if I could just believe that long enough to stop
caring about what happens with me

and you, I would.

I sometimes pour sand in mental mandalas.
I rub it around in geometric shapes, and colors
you'd be proud of.
But as the threat of wind begins to brush
against the wisps of my hair (it's getting longer now),
I frantically search for tarps, glass cases,

museum lobbies, security guards,
armies, navies, secret societies,
Gods. But the storm is coming anyway,
and I think I could bear it,
If I could see the face of God in your fingertips
like I used to.

yeah, yeah, we're all impressed you went to college once

Astral projections of invalid connections,
harmless pedantries.
Circular arguments don't solve 3-dimensional problems;
glassy eyed conversations don't invoke love.

I need you to see me (sober, or only two beers in) standing
under a waterfall (in the moss of course)
shirtless and stable,
and you would find it so charming.

Instead, I pour another beer,
sit on a weathered couch and
unsuccessfully fight off the urge
to widen the chasm between us.

Maybe if I had stepped across sooner,
or built a bridge along the way, I wouldn't be throwing notes
wrapped around stones, and watching
them fall into a Nietzschean
abyss that does nothing but stare back.

Parachute Hammock

Rocking silently in the dusk,

I almost hear the green leaves

shiver. Look up: sky

fragments, leafy stencils

that will soon be barren

twigs.

Does greenery feel the shift?

One day, waking up with a cough, unable

to get up as painlessly

as yesterday. Beginning to watch

friends and family fade

into a sea of yellow,

orange,

red.

They don't see their own hands, nervously twitching

into kaleidoscopes. Finally feeling

individual, unique, proud,

alone, as north winds get closer.

I hear them turning to God,

getting divorced, buying

a convertible. The birds have left

empty nests. Shiny red foil dangling

from one. Pretty decoration, like the

"homeiswheretheheartis"

picture frame in my parents' dining room.

As it gets dark I leave my hammocked paradise,

go into a house, cozy up to the fireplace,

ignore the chill in the air.

Simon and Garfunkel Stole This Title Before I Was Born (The Sound of Silence)

Tiny goldbrown fans circle

slowly to the ground. **"i was immature,**

I didn't know what it really

meant." She says as she

grinds a pine-cone passively,

eyes up, not seeing anything. I want

to reply, but there's nothing left

to say, so I say nothing. We sit in silence, and

try to feel the change in season. The moment

where warmth can officially be called

cool. We sit for 30 minute-hours, and find

that sometimes binaries

can't define, or save

anything.

Two Days Before My 25th Birthday

The precipitous nature of major

life decisions create a sensation

of drowning. A cold tingling

like panic attacks or altered

states, but I probably just need

to eat. Instead of decisions, it's just flipping

through photo albums, not the electronic

ones. Tangible pages with smells

and texture, and scope.

A realization of time as flat

and circular, and all things are

eternal. A permanent snapshot

of the last minute of our wedding night,

or the last time I heard you singing

to the dogs in the kitchen. All

encompassing, an existential nightmare

of tiny space and tiny time.

A free-will that only exists because

the way my synapses evolved to perceive

it. The comfort and agony of not knowing.

The path that always existed,

but can only be viewed in retrospect.

And as each fraction makes perception

of time speed into a horizon that is both

infinite and finite, I can't help but feel

like a B-list actor, improvising

a scene that the director finds going exactly

as planned.

And if time is all human perception, then I'm tracing

a photograph that has existed for eternity

and calling it movement, decisions,

"free-will." And if I could detach myself

from space and time, or time and space,

I wouldn't have to worry

about what happens next. I could just trace

and retrace 5 years, like re-reading

my favorite book, and getting something new

every time. Over and over and over.

Postcards

We were so tired in Boston

that we had a beer

with dinner and went to sleep at 9:30,

it was beautiful.

How the fuck did we end up at Walden Pond?

Thoreau has become a gift shop. I snuck a kiss

in Emerson's lended kitchen.

New York City

Timesquarepanicattack

We posed with imaginary twin towers,

thought about Bush reading

photo-ops to children.

In Florida we saw an osprey, it's claws

gouging a fish that was too big

to carry. The bird tried to take the prize home,

but sometimes even the best fish die

in the sand, and people like to watch.

Watering a Garden beside a Red Wheelbarrow

Porcelain teeth,

wonderland cats,

what you focus on is different than what is important.

Quirky hats with eyes and ears,

jackets with zipper faces,

all ask for affection from their tattooed mothers,

and the best of them willfully obliges.

I like the way you twist clear strings around dancing finger
bones in an attempt to control

poignant puppets in bland non-fiction.

Even perfect pastels

are cheapened versions

of the standard. I've seen you speak fantastic color wheel

conversations at a dinner party,

on a Friday night,

in the middle of June.

I only smoked a pipe for the first time once

The more I stare, the more sepia you become,

then you're Ansel Adams, and so am I.

And the most beautiful black and

white photograph I ever saw

Was you running toward

the phosphorescent prisms created by a front-

yard sprinkler

On a Sunday morning,

at the end of August.

Jay-Z Wrote a Song About This Period Of Life: "Less than 100 troubles, but…"

TM, TM, TM

"You're real! You're real! You're real!"
he repeats on records, or
should I say grainy
 iPhone (™) recordings,
in noise-cancelling headphones.

"Don't put so many technology references;
this shit will become dated quick."
He repeats at workshops, or
should I say in text boxes
on web-forums, like Blackboard (™).

"If the devil won the supposed war for heaven
wouldn't he also call himself God?"
He repeats at altars, or should
I say mumbles quietly as he watches a sermon
through his Macbook (™).

"It's just winter, everyone is sad in winter."
He repeats in conversations, or should I
say text messages with
his therapist. She says: "You just need
a little sunlight, or should I say a UV lamp (™)."

The Cosmic Hello (Or Therapist Conversation)

He molested us both, and Jamie is his nephew.

The moon is God's thumbnail tonight.

I didn't like the taste, but I didn't know what it was.

Karma's a bitch.

I'm afraid to talk to Jamie about it.

**Poseidon will wash this all away and start over
again.**

I don't really think it affects me on a conscious level.

**Nibiru is on a collision course with the sun, and
we're about to be set free.**

*Do you think my relationships will always be fucked on a
subconscious level?*

**The galaxy forms a double helix, the black hole
and the sun circling the toilet bowl of the
universe. We are all going to a place where light
doesn't exist, but we'll give into the intense
pressure far before that, and our bodies won't be
bodies anymore.**

Strangers

We called you queer,
but you were just comfortable
with yourself and we were in middle
school. How queer.

Last month your mom
went looking for you on
the streets of New York,
in alleyways and shelters.

And she found you, with a blanket
across your lap and a blunt
in your mouth. You told
her to go home, and she did.

My dad tells me about it and jokes,
"I wonder if he's sucking
dick for drugs." But my dad didn't say
that because he rarely curses and I'm a liar.

He said: "No telling what he's
doing to survive." And I wonder
if you are comfortable
with yourself. And if that's queer.

The Things I Shouldn't Write About

I'll drink your hands like fermented barley
as you tell me about your
        abortions, and your
        parents and your
        jewelry made out of insects and your
        ex-boyfriend that's not an ex-boyfriend at all.

My Bedroom Window

You can see the swimming pool from my bedroom window. You are right above it actually. You can see the whole backyard. There is a section of trees that is about 10 feet deep. I used to be afraid bears were going to come through the woods, climb up two stories, and break into my room. I can't say I'm very rational.

I spend a lot of time in my bedroom. I have a stereo with 3-disc rotation. I usually buy CDs 3 at a time and wear them out while I play video games.

You can see the swimming pool from my bedroom window. You can hear the shouts of my cousins as they run around the pool. You can hear the mumble of the adults on the porch talking while my dad cooks hamburgers that we will put on Wal-Mart white buns. He says, "They say white-wheat, so they must be healthy." Everyone is still alive. All the grandparents. All the aunts. All the uncles. All the cousins. Everyone still lives within 10 miles of each other. All the grandparents. All the aunts. All the uncles. All the cousins.

You can see the blinds of my bedroom window. You can see the window frame. Sometimes you can't see past that because it's too bright outside and the glare hurts the television. Sometimes when I hear "Ocean Avenue" by Yellowcard, I can remember what level on Tony Hawk Pro Skater 2 I was playing. My father and I have almost photographic memories. He tells me stories about playing kick the can on long car rides while I play my lime-green gameboy color.

You can see the swimming pool from my bedroom window. You can see the Fourth of July. You can see Labor Day. You can see Memorial Day. You can see family gathering around to spend time with one another. You can hear voices that I can't remember the exact pitch to, no matter how hard I try to run back the video recorder in my head. You can see faces that I forget the exact shape of until I'm reminded by a photograph. When I hear "Yourself or Someone Like You" by Matchbox 20, I can remember what level of Donkey Kong Country gave me the most trouble.

You can't see me in the swimming pool from my bedroom window. I'm still inside. I can turn my music up louder than normal because my parents are outside with my family. I ran down to grab a hamburger, some chips, and a Dr. Pepper, and now I'm set for hours. Aunt Corey lives in Alaska now; her son is in Nebraska; Uncle Kevin is is North Carolina now, or maybe Virginia; his sons are too; Papa has been dead for 10 years; I'm in Rhode Island. When I listen for their voices, I don't hear anything.

Norman Rockwell, 1964

Where is your happy family, Norman?
Steve is telling a racist
joke around a holiday turkey.

Carl is burning tiny crosses
to hang on the Christmas tree.
'Tis the season.

Faye's cheeks flush,
suppressing laughter, as
she blesses their hearts.

"Did you hear? They
are letting that
negro girl go to the white school?"

"Carl and I are going down
there to give them a
piece of our mind in the morning."

Steve's smile encapsulates
American dreams
on Christmas cards for 50 years.

Don't you dare forget
to remember
the good ol' days.

Jonathan's Soul-Group

Interdimensional beings
being transcendent with portals
and port-holes
and turtles.
Did you know the
oldest tortoise is 183 years
old? His name is
Jonathan.
He breathed
pre-industrial air
with his first
breath. And Jonathan
saw that
it was good. The first known
Jonathan was the
son of King Saul
who was later
known as Paul
after he saw a
blinding light. And
Paul saw that it
was good. Interdimensional
beings. Being transcendent
with portals, and
port-holes, and turtles.

Missing the Forest, and the Trees

Holy abacus!

Calculate every minutia!

Leave no stone un-

categorized!

Veil this like disappointed brides,

as they march and march

in perfect formation,

trying to emulate grown ugly

ducklings, flying south for winter.

(because of climate patterns in Asia)

Climb this mountain; don't look at the view,

but at the top look under your feet

with a microscope.

Tell me the granite percentage

of taking all of this for granted.

Tell me how sublime

the anatomy of an atom is.

You write a dissertation,

I'll paint a picture.

I'm going to put the word Dadaism in the Title

Gamma rays are eating the atmosphere as my computer screen eats code and spits out the urban

dictionary word of the day. As I learn a new synonym for "penis pump," I wonder absentmindedly about

Shakespeare and before making a connection to the advent of words, focus a little too long on the poofy

pants he's always wearing in my mind's eye. I sometimes wonder what Gandhi would think about yoga

pants and why "Free Bird" played alongside "I Believe I Can Fly" in a nonironic way at this funeral I

went to last month.

And why people die, when they are still busy being someone's husband, or father

And why the hell frosted tips came around in the 90s, and when they are coming back

And if Justin Timberlake is part of the illuminati

And if people will know I was joking about illuminati, but that I sometimes do believe conspiracies.

And if this is all just chaos,

And we are just created to grow up and die, or sometimes die before we grow up

Why do I care so much about who I eat breakfast with for the next 50 years?

And I wonder if Jesus liked the way sandals felt, or if they were the only things that were practical

And if geometrical shapes that occur in nature actually have different energies

And if my base chakra will ground me

And also if it will allow me to last longer in bed

And if I'm the only one that kind of gets turned on in a rainstorm

And if I'm not, if they will just eat breakfast with me sometimes.

Count backwards from 10. 'What is 10? Numbers are liars'

Your head is a shape-shifter

backwards baseball cap-

gun in your father's holster.

I don't know you

any better than I know myself.

Damn when did it get so cold,

shivers run from the base of my cerebellum.

I've heard LSD sometimes sits in your spinal cord,

reanimates itself at random futures.

"You're always listening to that depressing music"

Austin or the devil retorted to my panic.

And I don't want to go to the hell of Southern Baptist

reveren(ce)ds

I squeezed your dog for warmth

'til he yelped with fear.

The framerate of my eyes are laggy

pieceofshit components

lazy manufacturer

sound not matching picture

like Kung-Fu movies.

When I look at the sky I see mostly darkness

with scattered lights trying to illuminate

blank space and time

kaleidoscopic

but the darkness remains.

What is my constitution?

What is unalien?

able?

I've got knocking on every door of my perception

by demons and angels and Sylvia Plath.

And the voice I heard clearest sounded like my father

or my grandfather, in his straight jacket.

(to the ceiling to look underneath the hood)

I've got an eternity to figure out time

and place and how they are the same thing.

The impression I'm left with is just

jazz records

on vinyl

while my sister absent-mindedly picks at her DNA

with stubby fingers

like avoiding cheeseless nachos

from a haphazard concession.

"What do you hope to discover?"

I want to know

what remains

when entropy reaches zero.

Driving in Tunnels

Pass over double white lines in darkness.
Like climbing without rope supports.
Laying Face Up in A Door Frame
Like transmogrified car crash cumulus clouds
The safety of riding the fence.
The threshold between who I am, who I want to be, and
       who I inevitably will become
Slipping through portals, like driving through brick
       walls

"If gold rusts, what then can iron do?"

An ode to an art piece that is as alive as Thomas a Becket

Cross yourself to create
a visual of a cross right
in front of your face
or body
or spirit
or 3rd dimensional limits as a multidimensional being.

Flog yourself to remind
what you really fucking are:
a sinner
or a human
or a lover
or a trapped astral soul doomed to repeat, repeat, repeat.

Build structures to simulate
heaven, the great golden altar.
to kiss the feet of
or other cheek
or ass
or shiny molecules, bonded together until they are worthy.

Escape the room but not the house,
as Thomas' murdered soul
bounces around the cathedral
or floats away
or sings hallelujah
or never existed at all.

Fuck-It 18

A celebration of Shakespeare, probably...

At the end of every day you've spent a day.
"No shit," you say, trying to keep temperate.
Please, please, let me explain, if I may:
It does not matter, pick any single date,
April 21, 1995, what shines
to you that day? What has completely dimmed?
Is there something or someone who declines,
from your memory, left unburdened, untrimmed?
What about yesterday, what have you let fade?
It's not to me, but to yourself thou owe.
Even today, there are moments left in shade,
of trees seeded, you won't dare see grow.
We're all at a loss to what we truly see,
and keep, of what little is given to thee.

Tax Receipts from 1908 (or searching through a family heirloom)

An old trunk
full of out of focus
black and whites.
Smiles only captured
if they were forced. You
can almost see their
miasmas, cancers waiting
to activate, in that
old fashioned way, aurasmic
folds of brightness reflect
best in corners
of eyes.

People would have you
believe that reading them is all about
their color.
No.
No.
That's too categorical,
too linear
too third-dimensional.

"You really think ancestry matters?"
I'm as transcendent
as a cockroach hiding
in the corners of a bombed
out house, playing violin
and singing "Hallelujah" to no one
but the ashes, of the ashes
of my genetic confines.

Genre Undefined

I hear you are writing a new album
that mixes the sounds of leaves
crunching under gregarious
feet, the sound of water
rushing under foot-
bridges, and the worst mechanical
cacophonies you could make with
human hands. You wanted to see
at what point the nature noises
were stamped
out. You wanted to see how long
until you turned away in revulsion.
When the sounds were overtaken
completely? Or before?

Case of the Mondays

There was a homeless
man dancing
on the bridge overpass this morning
because the Patriots
won the Super Bowl
again. I let him pass over
me as I said 3 Hail Moneys
and drove underneath his bridge to work.

My Shortest Poem

There is a gift-shop at Walden pond.

The 4-Dimensional Texture of Time Feels A lot Like Sand

Butterflies and seagulls!

They're never in the same place in my imagination.

But they are now,

with my toes in the sand at Folly Beach.

they go together like opposite clichés.

If they are both (in a relative sense) far enough away

from me, they look the same size

on the ocean skyline,

like my sense of time when looking back on

old home movies.

Sometimes the wind makes them fly backwards,

and they beat and flutter for status quo, or worse.

Sometimes they embrace it.

Fly headlong into the future,

like they never have panic attacks about the constancy

of time and space.

And maybe happenstance blows them over some cat-

eyed sunset.

Sometimes they collide.

And the past eats the future--

leaves him wingless and dying on a tesseract

shoreline

wondering when the fuck the third dimension became

so damn obtuse.

I pour beer on top of him--

I hope it numbs him before I bury him in the sand.

Your Face Will Get Stuck Like That: A Villanelle for College Hipsters

Smoking a cigarette on the numbered streets
rings blow cancerous in the wind
against the dingy windows covered in sheets.

The corner is filled with tricks and treats,
and the empty promises of time well spent
smoking weed on the numbered streets.

I think of measurement in feats and feet,
as I write a bounced check for rent,
in the shadow of the dingy windows covered in sheets.

Across the street lives an artist who is neat,
next door a man in a tent,
he's smoking crack on the numbered streets.

In the middle I sit and bleat,
about the mind's creative covenant,
throw bricks through dingy windows covered in sheets.

It sticks in my throat like a record on repeat
When I say, "you'll drown in this current current."
So I just smoke a cigarette on the numbered streets,
blowing out dingy windows covered in sheets.

The Year Before I Changed Middle Schools

When I was 11 years
old there was a kid
at my lunch table who was having even more
social issues than I was. He had
ear wax built up
like he hoped the world would
one-day stop being so loud,
I pointed it
out for a deafening
laugh. Since then, every time
someone sits
beside me, I rub
my ears with dirty pinkies.
They're never looking.
 I'm never laughing.

"Be Cool" - Mick Jagger

Paint our faces
masquerade
honor holistic dance rituals.

Rightfootleftfoot
Gunshotstabwound
Rightfootleftfoot

Tap our feet to the beat,
nod our head to the rhythm
beat my friends with a bat.

"Peace,
Love,
Harmony"

San Franciscan monks
eat magic
mushrooms. Touch

each other.
Start a forest
fire. Kick each other.

in the fucking face.

Almost Real

I saw a sea shell
that looked like
a urinal cake. A cave
like a beer can with
the top popped off. A sunny
instagram post of
a sunny instagram
coast. And I know it's all
emulating
something, something, something.

Reflections

Karl Marx hasn't changed
in years. He just sits there smoking
a cigar, looking out the window
at abandoned factory lines. I've never seen him
so sad. He bites on the end of a pen,
with furrowed brow, until ink stains
his fingertips, his tongue, his shirt.
He sometimes asks what Marxism is. I spout
off other -isms that never quite define
the ideal, in a shallow attempt
to mirror Plato, but all I see are shadows
on shadows, a cave inside
a carnival funhouse.

Anaphoric Self-Portraits

Self, in abnormal hues
of blind quintessence.

Self, and self and self and
self in all its dream-like scrumtrulescent.

Self, in a purple
beanie and an unformed beard.

Self, a painting of a picture
off a posed candid mirror.

Self-
Actualization sipping wine in a coffee cup.

Self-
Reliance on a mind too corrupt.

New England New Me

Failed Attempts to Hula-Hoop

The darkness doesn't extend to sips of a shotgunned beer.

No, it can't touch me here.

Distance doesn't create anything sustainable, just

goodgoddamn electricity extending through fingertips

holyhallelujah goodnight kisses.

I would've sat up with you all night.

Maybe I did, in some other quantum universe

outside of space and time or time and space, where we are

meeting

and dancing

and screaming

broken harmonies into crowds and kissing

infinitely.

And that's beautiful in its own way, don't get me wrong,

but my faulty tape recorder brain is already losing the

edges of it all.

Don't get it twisted. I'm not saying I love you or anything,

but I have these blurry movies behind my eyes,

and I just want to watch them over, and over again.

Before the contact stops, and the memory fades,

before the daydream of seeing you again goes away,

before you and I cheapen the whole damn thing.

Gemini Nebulae and Blood Moons

Tracing backs of knuckles

like rubbing thumbs in a church pew.

Giving biographies to stomach rumblings,

this pillow talk is existential.

Cloud mountain ranges from plane windows,

dream images of your face while a kid kicks my chair.

Even the weather knows we are apart now, horoscopic

like something aligned stars today.

We are just beings of light thrust in frail frames.

I wonder if we came from the same star explosion.

Mingled together before humans had even evolved a false

sense of consciousness

and now, because light travels fast and hard

like my heart rate as I come back for one more kiss

just one more kiss

I just need one more kiss.

Shakespeare's Sonnets Didn't Have Titles, but This One Does

Vaudeville theatre, peg-legged statue,

two beers in on Tuesday trivia night.

Vagrant explaining his latin tattoo.

I'm just a key wrapped tight within a kite.

She and I. We. Staccatoed steps. One. Two.

I trace pictures, their distances' constraints

I'm always counting inches, me and you

and miles with broken keys and restraints.

And really it's not fair for me to dream

about quarter-Syrian locks of hair,

being let down in dark rooms, moans and screams.

The aftershock, the red curtain that tears

when she leaves on a jet plane once again.

She sips me in a flask she mixed with gin.

The Anxiety of 4 A.M. in Cambridge

Most of the universe is space

- Distances between objects

- Anti-matter

- Particles accelerating through blankness

Most of perception is time

- Distances between decisions

- past and future

I am damaged goods now because of

Two sets of paper:

- I dos

- I don'ts

Pretending to speak for souls with ink pens.

So the only question is, how strong is your will?

To let it sit here at one glimpse into the infinite

One shot of SoCo/no chaser

One hit of this sweetest drug

- In the rain

- In September

I won't move unless you ask me to

CLT to BOS

You sip me in a flask, mixed with gin,

With an emblazoned ram head insignia.

Stiff lipped swallow hides bitterness within,

As the plane throws shadows over Virginia.

You're drawing pictures of elephants and eyeballs

on the back of an off-white cocktail napkin.

You look down on freeways, houses, tall

buildings. You find them lacking.

You're bending worlds to the shape of your shaking hands,

Clay from the mountain ranges stuck under ocean fingernails.

Your firework eyes sparkle, constantly on the cusp of some grand

finale, and I'm watching every explosion to the last of its phosphorus trail.

You're a wildfire in a rainstorm, a clear stream in a drought,

And I'll always feed you kindling, siphon you into my mouth.

Hermetic

I only have interest in dawns
with you in them. Dew fresh
on overgrown lawns. We'll let
nature take its fingers
through flickers
of reality.

I want porch swing
Sundays, hands filled
with each other and spiked lemonade.

I want the broken breath passing back and forth
between broken
people. Red meeting shades of red
and red and red and red.
(The more times you say the word the less it means).

I will finish your sentences
and serve your sentences,
when you get incarcerated
by fragile bodies and missed
synapses.

I'm talking about lifetimes,
with parenthetical references,
innumerable is scribbles in the margins.
Peeling back layers of self
and self and self and self.

But me,
I can't get into your skin,

can't do anything about future hospital bands
or oblivion

Can't help but grow my beard long
and grey. Shaky hands over a
handmade cane, as I shuffle
feet through soul paths,
narrow ways that only fit one,
and one and one and one.

Written on A Sunny Day

I used to be enthralled by Paul Bunyan: The tale of the
man single-handedly taking on the

industrial revolution. The man strong enough to move
mountains, like some bastardized Old

Testament God.

There's something suffocating about space. The kind of
space where you see a

storm coming for half a day before it gets to you. You can't
enjoy the cloudless

sky above you on those days, because you know inevitably
the storm is coming. The inverse is

true, of course. I've been driving on a rainy day and looked
40 miles to my left to blue

skies in the neighboring town. This doesn't give you any
ease either. Just jealousy, impatience.

She said she woke up one morning from a dream and
everything was different. Like the

mountains of marriage had hidden the coming storm, and when they raged above us it was

already too late. Like the morning of your birthday when you notice a few frown lines

aren't fading. Something about the number going from 24 to 25 makes you linger in the

mirror a moment longer. I can't say if she's a liar or not.

Every tree I've ever seen on hikes in the North Carolina mountains are less than 100 years old.

This is a result of clear-cutting around the turn of the 20th century. It's in our nature to destroy in

order to create. There are more houses and people on the earth than ever before.

I said, "You can't control your feelings, but you can control your actions."

She said, "I don't want to be controlled at all."

She was an officiant of her friend's wedding. They jokingly called her "voodoo priestess". The

next day she told me "I don't believe in marriage."

Sometimes it takes a long drive to clear your mind properly. Sometimes creating distance is

the only way to feel the way your brain knows you should have felt a long time ago.

It was raining. I poked holes in all my umbrellas and complained about

getting wet. I looked 40 miles to my left and saw clear skies. I've never seen clouds move so

slow.

Some days I looked up and the sky had cleared. I looked to the right and left and felt

suffocating space. I didn't see any clouds on the horizon, but I felt them beyond the edge of

the world. I couldn't forget for a moment that the world is round.

Sometimes I'm afraid I won't ever forget my raincoat again. No matter how warm the world

gets. No matter how good the weather report is. I'm going to pack it in my bag anyway.

Before automobiles were invented, most people never traveled more than 50 miles from the

place they were born. Before planes were invented, 1000 miles was at least one day's journey.

I love that 80's song that talks about walking 500 miles for love. I only listened to it before I met you,

now I hear it.

I know it's selfish, but I'm enjoying the drought we've been having. I haven't worn my

raincoat in months, but I make sure to pack it, just in case.

Most people you meet from 16 to 22 are disposable. I read that on Tumblr. Credit: the

open forum of the Internet.

I noticed my first grey hair the same day I noticed the first grey hair on my dog's muzzle. I fall

asleep on the couch with him at least once a week. He tries to emulate police sirens when they

race by my house. I sometimes wonder what they are saying to him.

The first time I forgot my rain jacket was when you visited me in South Carolina. I didn't tell

you then. I was still too afraid.

I read a quote that said something similar to: the problem with this world is that too many

people say "I love you" just to hear it back.

The record high for today was posted in 1908. It was 78 degrees. Today didn't quite make it.

Today, I burned my rain jacket and you said the flame was beautiful. I barely glanced at it

before making a corny joke.

You once accidentally told me you loved me on a couch, while we mused over

breaking the chains society puts on us. We were watching *Into the Wild*. You said you loved

gentle old men whose energy doesn't match their age. "And of course you." You said that on accident.

I love waterfalls, rain storms, feeling like you'd never let me drown in too much water.

Oh, and of course you. I said that on purpose.

Dread Pirate Roberts

"This is true love. You think this happens every day?"

This isn't one of those kissing books.

This is about inevitability.

It's been a year at sea, and God I'm just ready to come

home.

I grow tired of blazing turrets, black masts.

I just want to burn this mask in your fires,

so you, and only you, can see what's underneath.

I've sent fear and doubt on planks in shark infested waters,

I've got no need for those.

And you, you don't need to be rescued,

except from space and time.

This is coming-of-age.

Transitioning from war to peace,

preferring happy endings to gritty realism.

But people don't get happy endings.

"Nonsense. You're only saying that because no one ever

has."

I will not settle for less than shared sunsets

uncountable, but always too few.

Jalapenos

You're trying to stonewall
me. Scare me away
with your heat. I've burned my tongue on
so many cups of coffee it's lost
its sensitivity. I will bite into
your crisp, green skin. Let your seeds
stick in my throat until I cough
tears. You thought this would keep
me away. But burning fires
do more than destroy
wooden houses.

The Things We Make with Our Hands

I want to grow a tree out of my chest

gnarled roots as veins, ventricles.

I want to brew my coffee with soil,

French press, not those drip machines.

I want to bear fruit

that children suck between teeth

when they take a 5-minute break

from playing hide and seek.

I want you to build a home in me

With leaves and twigs and broken things

I want you to feel secure

on clear starry nights

or when the storms threaten to topple me

over.

'Cause baby I won't break,

won't be destroyed by happenstance.

And when this is done,

you can chop me down,

count the rings and stories I made for

myself

and for you.

Pour the sap in syrup bottles

so you have something sweet with your

breakfast.

Build foundations with me

and let every knot that splinters your

front porch,

every imperfection,

be understood in the way only you can.

You can knock on me to ward off bad luck

and I'll always be your cool shade in

summer.

Audience

Sometimes I say what
I mean, but
mostly I write
poetry
to you bringing me
back home
to when
I wished I
was where I am now.

I've seen puddles
become ice become
puddles again now
that I live in New England
but I've only
seen coats thrown
on them in movies and metaphors.
And I can't help
but think, no one
is interested in my love notes,
these water-cover coats,
except everyone who's written
a love note. And you.

Made in the USA
Middletown, DE
16 July 2018